the marriage course

> Leaders' Guide

First published 2001

Revised 2004

This revised edition 2009

ISBN: 978 1 905887 46 0

Published by Alpha International, Holy Trinity Brompton, Brompton Road, London SW7 1JA.
publications@alpha.org

Contents

Welcome

We're so glad that you've decided to run The Marriage Course and we hope you enjoy the experience as much as we do. We've run it three times a year since 1996, and we love it! For us, the greatest satisfaction comes from seeing the couples' relationships being strengthened, and in some cases, transformed over the eight sessions.

This *Leaders' Guide* is designed as a quick reference. We find it really helpful to have it with us when we are running a session. The checklists and timetables are particularly useful and help keep us on track.

For training and additional in-depth information on how to run the course, we suggest you get hold of *The Marriage Course Leaders' Toolkit*. This has lots of helpful advice on setting up, running and publicising a course.

Please do contact us if you have any questions and do let us know how you get on. We love to hear feedback from other courses.

Nicky and Sila

Nicky and Sila Lee
Creators of The Marriage Course

Introduction

The Marriage Course was started at Holy Trinity Brompton, London, in 1996 and the material was first published in 2001. Since then, thousands of other courses have started around the world. The second edition of the course was produced on DVD with updated manuals in 2009.

The course is for any married or cohabiting couple, whether they've been together for one year or sixty-one years, whether they have a good relationship or are struggling. The practical tools of the course are applicable to everyone.

The course is made up of seven sessions with The Marriage Course Party at the end, when couples can invite their friends to find out more about the course.

There is also an optional session called 'Coping with Times of Separation', created for those in the armed forces and other couples who have to spend extended time apart.

Each session ideally starts with a meal, as this gives guests a chance to relax and talk to their partner in a romantic setting. Creating a great atmosphere is an important part of the course, as is the assurance that there are no group discussions. Many people would be put off coming to a course if they thought they might have to share intimate details of their relationship with other people (or if they thought their partner might be given the opportunity to share intimate details of their relationship with other people!).

After the meal, the leaders welcome the guests, give any notices and do a quick review of the last session. They then either give the talks live, or show the DVD.

During each session there are breaks in the talks to give the couples an opportunity to discuss some of the issues that have been raised. The couples are spread far enough apart, and background music is played, to ensure their discussions are not overheard.

How to run the course

The course is designed to be very easy to run, whether you give the talks live or use the DVDs. If it's your first time running the course we would recommend using the DVDs as this means you can concentrate on hosting and creating the right atmosphere.

Whichever way you decide to run the course, you will need to provide a guest manual for each person. These contain the exercises that the couples do during and after each session.

The Marriage Course Leaders' Toolkit is highly recommended for any leader or potential leader. It will give you lots of helpful tips and advice on getting going successfully.

Using the DVDs

All the sessions of the course are available on DVD. Nicky and Sila's talks were filmed in a TV studio and each session includes street interviews from around the world, sofa couples (married couples talking about their experiences of marriage) and a feature couple who give a more in-depth interview on a particular topic.

The DVDs indicate when to pause for an exercise break. You'll also see the timings of these listed in the timetable for each session on pages 16–32 of this guide.

Top tip:
Using the DVDs allows you to focus on hosting and creating a great atmosphere.

Giving live talks

If you are giving the talks yourselves, the *Leaders' Toolkit* is an invaluable resource. It includes:

- speakers' transcripts with guidance notes
- filmed inserts (sofa couples, street interviews and the feature couples) for you to include in your talks
- instructions in the transcript that indicate when each filmed insert should be shown

NB: there are more 'sofa couple' inserts for each session than you will have time to include if you are giving live talks. We've indicated in the transcript which inserts we consider the most helpful and which ones could be omitted.

Preparation suggestions for live talks

- watch the DVD of the particular session. You may also want to read the relevant section of *The Marriage Book*
- decide who will do each section of the talk, ensuring that you both have a turn to speak
- agree on what stories you are going to share from your own marriage
- adjust the speakers' transcripts (found on the CD-ROM of the *Leaders' Toolkit*) adding illustrations from your own marriage

Structure of a typical evening session

for Sessions 1–7

The whole session, including the meal, lasts approximately two-and-a-half hours but can be shortened by reducing the length of the talks. We strongly suggest that you do not shorten the length of the exercises as these are the most beneficial aspect of the whole course. Pages 16–32 include timings for each session.

1. Welcome

Some guests are apprehensive on the first evening so a drink and a warm welcome help them to feel relaxed.

2. The meal (30 minutes)

Many people who have done the course have commented that the meal has made it feel like a 'date night'.

Top tip:
Men in particular can be hesitant about coming on the course so having other men to welcome them can make a big difference.

3. Notices and review (up to 10 minutes)

We recommend beginning with brief notices, and then giving couples the opportunity to review the previous session(s).

4. Talks and short exercises

The talks are interspersed with exercises and opportunities for husband and wife to talk to one another. (Each short exercise lasts between 5–10 minutes.) Background music should be played to ensure conversations are not overheard. The DVDs and the speakers' transcripts (in the *Leaders' Toolkit*) as well as the timetables in this guide provide details of the timing and length of the exercises.

5. Feature couple (5 minutes)

Each session of the DVD includes a 'feature couple' – a short film featuring a married couple who share about the impact The Marriage Course has had on their relationship. With the talks as an alternative to showing the feature couple DVD from the *Leader's Toolkit*, you could ask a couple who have been guests on a previous course to talk about the difference this particular session has made in their own marriage. Interviewing them enables the leader to guide what they say and to limit the length, if necessary. Both husband and wife should speak. We suggest finding out beforehand what difference the session made to their marriage and asking questions that will keep the testimony personal. Some potential questions are:

- why did you come on The Marriage Course?
- what happened for each of you during this session?
- what difference has it made in your relationship?

6. Long exercise (30–35 minutes)

To ensure privacy, provide each couple with their own table/space and play background music. Coffee, tea and dessert are served by the leaders and volunteers.

7. Conclusion

Guests are encouraged to arrange 'marriage time' for the coming week. From Session 3 onwards, they are given the opportunity either to pray for their husband or wife, or to express their support for each other in some other way. The leaders finish the evening with a short prayer (from the DVD, or live).

8. Feedback

A questionnaire is available for distribution during Session 7 (see CD-Rom of the *Leaders' Toolkit*). This serves as a review of the course for the guests and provides helpful feedback for the leaders.

Four tips for creating a great atmosphere

A warm and welcoming environment is very important to the success of the course. It is essential that guests feel relaxed and that they are able to talk with their partner about sensitive issues; a great atmosphere ensures this is possible. (See *Leaders' Toolkit* for more ideas.)

1. Choose the best venue

The key is to find a location that allows you to create a welcoming atmosphere and serve a meal:

- if you have less than five couples, a home is usually the best location
- larger courses can be held in a church hall, restaurant, café after hours, hotel, etc. Even the most uninspiring room can be turned into a great venue with a little creativity

> ***Top Tip:***
> *The Leaders' Toolkit contains some recommended music to help create a great atmosphere and ensure couples' conversations are not overheard.*

2. **Think romantic date night: intimate, cosy, special**

- if the course is not held in a home and the space is uninspiring, find someone who enjoys the challenge of transforming it to look welcoming, relaxed and romantic
- small tables for two, spaced sufficiently far apart, are ideal as they give each couple a sense of privacy during discussion times
- low lighting and soft background music during the meal and exercises help to create the 'date night' atmosphere

3. **Provide food**

- serving a meal before the course gives guests the opportunity to unwind and catch up. It also means people can come straight from work without having to worry about eating before the course
- meal timing – we recommend serving the main course at the start of each session. Coffee, tea and a simple dessert can then be served during the long exercise break later in the evening

4. **Give great service**

- some couples worry about coming on The Marriage Course and it really helps to have a friendly team who go out of their way to make the guests feel welcome
- it's a great idea if the leaders can help serve the coffee and tea in the long break. This helps show the couples that you care about them and that their relationship is important to you

Quick checklist

For all courses (whether using the DVDs or giving live talks)

- ☐ This *Leaders' Guide*
- ☐ *The Marriage Course DVD* set (for those using the filmed talks)
- ☐ *Guest Manuals* (one per person)
- ☐ Music (and a way to play it) – to be used during the meal, discussions and at the end of each session
- ☐ Food (meal, cold drinks, coffee, tea and dessert)
- ☐ Tables and chairs, suitable lighting, tablecloths, table napkins, candles, flowers and vases
- ☐ Plates, glasses, cups and cutlery
- ☐ Attendance list and name labels
- ☐ Spare pens and *Guest Manuals* (in case guests forget theirs)

> ***Top Tip:***
> *You may want to have a copy of The Marriage Book (by Nicky and Sila Lee) to give to couples who want to follow up on a particular session.*

- [ ] Book table (if you want to display some recommended books)
- [ ] Speakers' stand and microphone (for larger groups)
- [ ] Spare DVDs of each session for couples who may have missed a session (these can be loaned with a deposit so they can be replaced if not returned)
- [ ] DVD player
- [ ] TV or screen and projector

Additional items for those giving live talks

- [ ] The speakers' transcripts (from the *Leaders' Toolkit*)
- [ ] The filmed inserts DVD for the session (from the *Leaders' Toolkit*)
- [ ] PowerPoint or overhead projector for displaying diagrams from the *Leaders' Toolkit* (optional)
- [ ] A feature couple to interview for 5 minutes about their experiences of The Marriage Course (if not using the recorded couples on the filmed inserts DVD in the *Leader's Toolkit*)

NB: Please also review the checklists included in 'Overview and timetable for each session' beginning on page 16 for additional items you may need for each session.

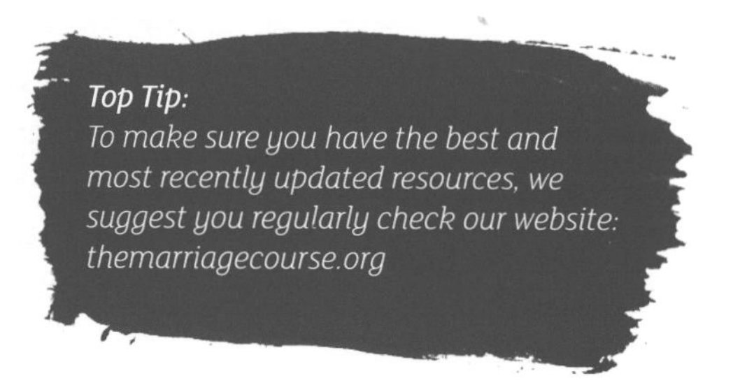

Session 1 – Building Strong Foundations

1. Overview

This session helps couples to look at their lifestyle and the effect it has on their marriage, and to discover more about each other's needs and desires – particularly on an emotional level.

2. Checklist

- materials from Quick checklist on pages 14–15
- visual aids (for live talks only): sheets of coloured paper (separate and stuck together)

3. Timetable

6.30 Be ready! (Guests often arrive early)

6.45 Welcome and drinks

7.00 Meal

7.25 5 minute warning

7.30 Welcome and notices

- *'If you get stuck at any point on the course, please tell us'*
- *'We or another couple would be very happy to see you privately. We also have details of a local marriage counsellor we could put you in touch with if you feel this is necessary'*
- *'Let us know if you can't come for one of the evenings and we will loan you the DVD'* (if available)
- *'Relax! You will not be required to disclose anything private about your relationship'*

Note: The following timings follow the exact timings of the length of the talks on the DVDs.

7.35 Start the DVD or your live talk – Introduction

7.44 Exercise 1 (5 minutes) –*The First Time You Met: 'Tell each other your strongest memory of the first time you met and what first attracted you to one another'*

7.49 Talk – *What is marriage?*
Live talks: first part of demonstration – hold together two separate pieces of paper

7.54 Talk – *Seasons of marriage*
Live talks: second part of demonstration – try to separate two pieces of paper glued together

8.12 Exercise 2 (5 minutes) – *Working Through Pressures: 'Talk together about the pressures you've worked through until now in your relationship, and the pressures you're currently facing. Take it in turns to listen to each other'*

8.17 Talk – *Marriage wheel and overview of sessions*
Feature Couple: Doug and Angela (from *Leaders' Toolkit* filmed inserts – Session 1 Insert 23) or your own feature couple

8.28 Exercise 3 (30 minutes) – *Taking Stock of Your Marriage*

8.53 Give a 5 minute warning

8.58 Talk – *Making time for each other*

9.08 Exercise 4 (5 minutes) – *Shared Times: 'Tell your partner what have been the most special times you have shared together as a couple. Be specific about when, where and what you were doing. Explain why they were special to you'*

9.13 Talk – *Nurturing one another*

9.18 Exercise 5 (10 minutes) – *Knowing Me, Knowing You*

9.28 Conclusion – Encourage couples to bring diaries or calendars each week to book in marriage time

9.31 Live talks: End with a short prayer. For example:
'Thank you, Lord, that you are the God of love, the God who created marriage for us. We ask that you would help us to grow in our understanding of each other and to recognise each other's needs so that our love would deepen. We ask this in Jesus' name. Amen'

Session 2 – The Art of Communication

1. Overview

Listening is a vital skill for a strong marriage. In this session couples practise communicating their feelings and listening effectively to one another.

2. Checklist

- materials from Quick checklist on pages 14–15
- for leaders' demonstration of *Effective Listening* (for live talks only): an issue to discuss, two chairs, a table napkin or handkerchief (to be held by the speaker)

3. Timetable

6.45 Welcome guests with a drink

7.00 Meal

7.25 5 minute warning

7.30 Notices and review

- *Remind couples of the importance of 'marriage time' and understanding each other's emotional needs and desires*
- *'Without looking in your manual, tell your husband or wife their top three desires from the exercise in Session 1 – Knowing Me, Knowing You – to see if you have remembered them correctly'*
- *'Find out from your husband or wife what was most important for them from Session 1'*

7.40 Start the DVD or your live talk – Introduction – *Effective communication*

7.53 Exercise 1 (5 minutes) – *Barriers to Talking*

7.58 Talk – *Importance of listening*

8.00 Exercise 2 (5 minutes) – *The Power of Listening*

8.05 Talk – *Hindrances to listening: filters and bad habits*

8.20 Exercise 3 (4 minutes) – *Identifying Bad Habits*

8.24 Talk – *Hindrances to listening (continued)*

8.26 Exercise 4 (6 minutes) – *A Significant Memory*

8.32 Talk – *Five steps for effective listening*

8.37 Live talks: Leaders' demonstration of effective listening:

- *One of you needs to have thought of an issue that you would like to discuss. (Do not choose an issue that would be hurtful or embarrassing to discuss in front of others)*
- *The speaker holds the handkerchief or table napkin to remind both of you whose issue it is*
- *Using the five principles for effective listening, demonstrate what effective listening looks like (as on DVD)*

8.43 Exercise 5 (30 minutes) – *Effective Listening*

9.08 Give 5 minute warning

9.13 Feature Couple: Richard and Zoe (from *Leaders' Toolkit* filmed inserts – Session 2 Insert 23) or your own feature couple

9.18 Conclusion – Give 3 minutes to organise marriage time for the coming week

9.21 Live talks: End with a short prayer. For example:
'Lord, thank you that you are a God who communicates with us. Thank you that we can pour out our hearts to you and you always listen to us. Please help us to be good at expressing our feelings and listening to each other so that we may grow in our understanding and support of one another. We ask this in Jesus' name. Amen'

Session 3 – Resolving Conflict

1. Overview

In this session we look at how couples can increase their intimacy by expressing appreciation to each other, recognising their differences, learning to negotiate disagreements and praying for each other (if they feel comfortable doing so).

2. Checklist

- materials from Quick checklist on page 14–15

3. Timetable

6.45 Welcome guests with a drink

7.00 Meal

7.25 5 minute warning

7.30 Notices and review

- *'Tell your husband or wife one occasion over this last week when they met one of your requests from Knowing Me, Knowing You (Session 1, Exercise 2)'*
- *'Tell your husband or wife what it felt like to be listened to during the Effective Listening exercise in Session 2'*

7.40 Talk – Introduction – *Expressing our appreciation of each other*

7.53 Exercise 1 (10 minutes) – *Showing Appreciation*

8.03 Talk – *Identify and accept our differences*

8.14 Exercise 2 (10 minutes) – *Recognising Your Differences*

8.24 Talk – *Learn to negotiate*
Feature couple: Henrik and Inger (from *Leaders' Toolkit* filmed inserts –Session 3 Insert 23) or your own feature couple

8.49 Exercise 3 (30 minutes) – *Matching Our Strides*

9.14 Give a 5 minute warning

9.19 Talk – *Learning to pray together*

9.30 Conclusion – *Supporting each other*

The couples ask their partner to tell them one thing they are concerned about. Then, give them the option:

- either to pray for each other (aloud or silently) if they feel comfortable doing so
- or to express their support in some other way

9.34 Live talks: End with a short prayer. For example:

'And so we know and rely on the love God has for us" (1 John 4:16). 'Thank you Lord that you know each one of us intimately and that you love us as we are. Thank you for the uniqueness of each person here tonight and for the partnerships that have come into being in each marriage. We pray you would help us to grow together and to support each other effectively.

And please fill us with your love that we might be strengthened in our love for each other. We ask this in Jesus' name. Amen'

Encourage couples to organise marriage time for the coming week

Session 4 – The Power of Forgiveness

1. Overview

This session addresses the ways we will inevitably hurt each other and how to resolve these issues in order to ensure we don't create a backlog of anger and resentment. We look at the process of healing through identifying the hurt, saying sorry and forgiving.

2. Checklist

- materials from Quick checklist on pages 14–15
- visual aid (for live talks only): spiral-bound notebook to tear off pages symbolising forgiveness

3. Timetable

6.45 Welcome guests with a drink

7.00 Meal

7.25 5 minute warning

7.30 Notices and review

- *Review of Sessions 1–3 – 'Tell your husband or wife which point from the reminder section in the manual you consider the most important for your marriage at the moment'*
- *'Discuss whether over the past two weeks you have managed to work through problems together rather than attacking and criticising each other'*

7.40 Talk – *Dealing with hurt and anger (rhinos and hedgehogs)*

7.56 Exercise 1 (NB: 1 minute) – *Rhinos and Hedgehogs – identify yourself and your partner as a rhino or a hedgehog*

7.57 Talk – *Effects of hurt and anger*

7.59 Exercise 2 (10 minutes) – *Handling Anger*

8.09 Talk – *Process for healing hurt (part 1)*
1. Identify the hurt
2. Say sorry

8.31 Exercise 3 (35 minutes) – *Identifying Unresolved Hurt*

9.01 Give a 5 minute warning

9.06 Talk – *Process for healing hurt (part 2)*
3. Forgive
Feature couple: Andy and Vanessa (from *Leaders' Toolkit* filmed inserts – Session 4 Insert 19) or your own feature couple
Live talks: demonstration with spiral notebook
4. Start again together

9.24 Conclusion (4 minutes) – Give couples the opportunity to pray for their husband or wife or to express support in some other way

9.28 Live talks: End with a short prayer. For example:
'Lord, thank you for your willingness to forgive us. Thank you for your example and for bearing the cost of our forgiveness on the cross. We ask you to help us to forgive each other and to keep no record of each other's wrongs. We pray that you would heal our marriage of the ways we've hurt one another. We ask this in Jesus' name. Amen'

Encourage couples to organise marriage time for the coming week

Session 5 – The Impact of Family – Past and Present

1. Overview

This session focuses on helping couples to recognise how their family background affects the way they relate to each other. They also consider how to build a good, healthy relationship with their parents, in-laws and wider family, and how hurt from childhood can be healed.

2. Checklist

- materials from Quick checklist on pages 14–15
- visual aid: small bag of spare coins (for the exercise *Reflect on Your Upbringing*)

3. Timetable

6.45 Welcome guests with a drink

7.00 Meal

7.25 5 minute warning

7.30 Notices and review

- *Encourage couples to ask for help if they get stuck over an issue that the course has raised*
- *Review of sessions 1–4 – 'Looking at this week's reminder section in the manual, tell your partner either, "You're good at..." or, "I need to..." but not, "You need to...".'*

7.40 Talk – Introduction – *Impact of upbringing*
Stages of growing up

8.01 Exercise 1 (6 minutes) – *Current Relationships: Each couple discusses wider family relationships and identifies tensions*

8.07 Talk – *Building healthy family relationships*
Feature couple: David and Joy (from *Leaders' Toolkit* filmed inserts – Session 5 Insert 19) or your own feature couple

8.25 Exercise 2 (10 minutes) – *Building Healthy Family Relationships: 'Discuss which are the most relevant points for you from this exercise'*

8.35 Talk – *Looking at our past*

8.42 Exercise 3 (30 minutes) – *Reflect on Your Upbringing* – supply coins (if needed) to arrange and draw around

9.07 Give a 5 minute warning

9.12 Talk – *Healing childhood pain*
1. Recognise unmet childhood needs
2. Grieve with each other
3. Forgive
4. Look to God and move on

9.24 Conclusion (4 minutes) – Give couples the opportunity to pray for their husband or wife or to express support in some other way

9.28 Live talks: End with a short prayer. For example:
'Lord, thank you for your plans for family life. We pray that where a family background has affected a marriage, you would bring your love and understanding between them as a couple. Please give them new courage and new hope. Teach all of us to be gentle with one another. And we ask you to help those who have been hurt to trust you for your healing love. We ask this in Jesus' name. Amen'

Encourage couples to organise marriage time for the coming week

Session 6 – Good Sex

1. Overview

Sexual intimacy needs to be worked at and developed. It isn't just the icing on the cake; it's a vital ingredient of the cake itself. In this session couples are encouraged to talk about their sexual relationship and to recognise where they need to make changes.

Leaders who give their own talks need to be able to talk about this subject without embarrassment and with some gentle humour.

2. Checklist

- materials from Quick checklist on pages 14–15
- The Marriage Course Party invitations

3. Timetable

6.45 Welcome guests with a drink

7.00 Meal

7.25 5 minute warning

7.30 Notices and review

- *Encourage guests to invite other couples to the party (Session 8) at the end of the course. Explain what will happen on the evening*
- *'Talk as a couple about what was most important for you from the last session on the impact of family – past and present'*

7.40 Talk – Introduction

7.44 Talk – *Six qualities for great lovers*
1. Communication

8.03 Feature couple: Richard & Katharine (from *Leaders' Toolkit* filmed inserts – Session 6, Insert 12) or your own feature couple

8.07 Exercise 1 (5 minutes): *'Discuss what elements of this talk have been most relevant to you and your partner'*

8.12 Talk – *Six qualities (continued)*
2. Tenderness
3. Responsiveness
4. Romance

8.26 Exercise 2 (6 minutes): *'Tell each other the most romantic times you have had together'*

8.32 Talk – *Six qualities (continued)*
5. Anticipation
6. Variety

8.42 Exercise 3 (35 minutes) – *Talking About Sex*

9.12 Give a 5 minute warning

9.17 Talk – *Protecting our marriage*

9.25 Conclusion (4 minutes) – Give couples the opportunity to pray for their husband or wife or to express support in some other way

9.28 Live talks: End with a short prayer. For example:
'Lord, we thank you for the way you have made us with all the complexity and subtlety of our sexual desires and responses. Thank you that we are able to express love to each other through being joined together sexually. Help us as we learn to arouse each other and then to satisfy those desires. Help us to give ourselves to each other in love throughout our marriage. We ask this in Jesus' name. Amen'

Encourage couples to organise marriage time for the coming week

Session 7 – Love in Action

1. Overview

This session looks at five ways of expressing love – through words, time, touch, presents and actions. Couples discover which expression of love is most important for their partner and how to put this into practice.

2. Checklist

- materials from Quick checklist on pags 14–15
- end of course questionnaire – see sample on the *Leaders' Toolkit* CD-Rom
- Marriage Course Party invitations
- invitations to the next Marriage Course
- presents for your volunteer 'taskforce'

3. Timetable

6.45 Welcome guests with a drink

7.00 Meal

7.25 5 minute warning

7.30 Notices and review

- *Remind the guests of the opportunity to invite other married couples to The Marriage Course Party*
- *Encourage the guests to take invitations to the next Marriage Course to give to others*
- *'We have spoken about the difference that it makes to us to have God at the centre of our marriage. If you would like to explore the Christian faith further, there is a course called Alpha. You would be very welcome to come on the next Alpha course.' Put Alpha invitations out at the back*
- *'Please would each of you fill in the questionnaire. This acts as a review of the course for you and is very helpful for us'*

7.45 Talk – Introduction – *Five ways to express love*
1. Loving words
2. Thoughtful presents

8.11 Exercise 1 (6 minutes) – *Favourite Presents: 'Tell each other what have been the best presents you have received from each other'*

8.17 Talk – *Five ways to express love (continued)*
3. Physical affection
4. Quality time

8.29 Exercise 2 (10 minutes) – *Time Together: 'Make a list of the things you and your partner most enjoy doing together or would like to do together'*

8.39 Talk – *Five ways to express love (continued)*
5. Kind actions
Feature couple: Paul and Sonja (from *Leaders' Toolkit* filmed inserts – Session 7 Insert 26) or your own feature couple

8.50 Exercise 3 (30 minutes) – *Discovering Your Own and Your Partner's Love Languages*

9.15 Give a 5 minute warning

9.20 Talk – *The importance of commitment*

9.29 Conclusion (4 minutes) – Give couples the opportunity to express their commitment to their future together and then either to pray for each other or to express their support in some other way

9.33 Live talks: Read the prayer of St Francis of Assisi and then end with another short prayer. For example:
'Lord, we thank you for the power of love. Thank you that your love never fails. We pray that you would bless each marriage and use each couple to be a source of love and encouragement to many others. And we ask that in our marriages love and faithfulness would meet together. We ask this in Jesus' name. Amen'

Ask the guests to complete the questionnaire and hand it in before they leave

The Marriage Course Party

1. Overview

The aim is for the guests on the course to invite other couples to hear about The Marriage Course and to learn something that will benefit their relationship. The meal is longer, the talk is shorter than for the other sessions and there are no exercises. The party is a very effective way of introducing couples to The Marriage Course, as many people are initially more likely to come to one evening with a talk about marriage than to join a course. Many of the party guests subsequently do The Marriage Course.

Note: You will need more volunteers to help with this session due to the additional guests and serving the meal.

2. Checklist

- materials from Quick checklist on pages 14–15
- larger tables (for about 8–10 people each)
- invitations to the next Marriage Course
- centrepieces for each table
- decorations

3. Timetable

7.00 Welcome guests with a drink

7.30 Meal

8.10 Give a 5 minute warning

8.15 Welcome and introduction

8.20 Talk – *What makes a marriage grow?*

8.50 Testimonies by 3 or 4 couples who are on the current course** (if not using *Leaders' Toolkit* filmed inserts – Session 8 Insert 12)

9.00 Conclusion – Guests are served coffee or tea and given an invitation to the next Marriage Course

** The end of course questionnaires can help you select the testimony couples. Have a balance of couples who have been married for a shorter/longer length of time, who have/do not have children/whose children have left home, who have a strong marriage/who were experiencing difficulties in their marriage, so that each guest can relate to at least one of the testimony couples.

Extra session: Coping with Times of Separation

1. Overview

This session is designed particularly for those in the armed forces to help them cope with times of separation and the added challenges and pressures they face, especially when a partner goes into a combat zone. It will also be helpful to other couples who spend extended time apart as a result of illness or some other reason.

2. Checklist

- materials from Quick checklist on pages 14–15

3. Timetable

6.45 Welcome guests with a drink

7.00 Meal

7.25 5 minute warning

7.30 Talk – Introduction

7.38 Exercise 1 (5 minutes): *'How has separation affected your relationship or how do you think it will affect you?'*

7.43 Talk – *The emotional cycle of deployment*
Stage 1: Anticipation of loss

7.55 Exercise 2 (5 minutes) – *'How will you protect your relationship from temptation while apart?'*

8.00 Talk – *Stage 1: Anticipation of loss (continued)*
Stage 2: Detachment and withdrawal

8.10 Exercise 3 (15 minutes) – *Separation Evaluation*

8.25 Talk – *Stage 3: Immediate effects of separation*
Stage 4: Establishing a new routine
Stage 5: Anticipation of homecoming

8.38 Exercise 4 (5 minutes) – *'What do you look forward to most about your reunion?'*

8.43 Talk – *Stage 6: Renegotiating roles and responsibilities*

8.56 Exercise 5 (25 minutes) – *Identifying roles and how separation affects these*

9.16 Give a 5 minute warning

9.21 Talk – *Establishing normal life together*

9.27 Live talks: End with a short prayer. For example:
'A verse in the Old Testament says, "A cord of three strands is not quickly broken," and describes the strength of a marriage with God at the centre. So we'd like to pray for you now: 'Lord we thank you for your promise to be with us wherever we are. We pray for each couple who is facing times of separation, that they would know they are not alone when they are apart from each other and that with your strength they would cope with the difficulties and temptations that they face.

'Please guide them and help them to grow in their understanding of each other so that their marriage would not only survive these times, but would become closer and stronger through them. We ask this in Jesus' name. Amen'

Encourage couples to organise marriage time for the coming week

Suggested room set up

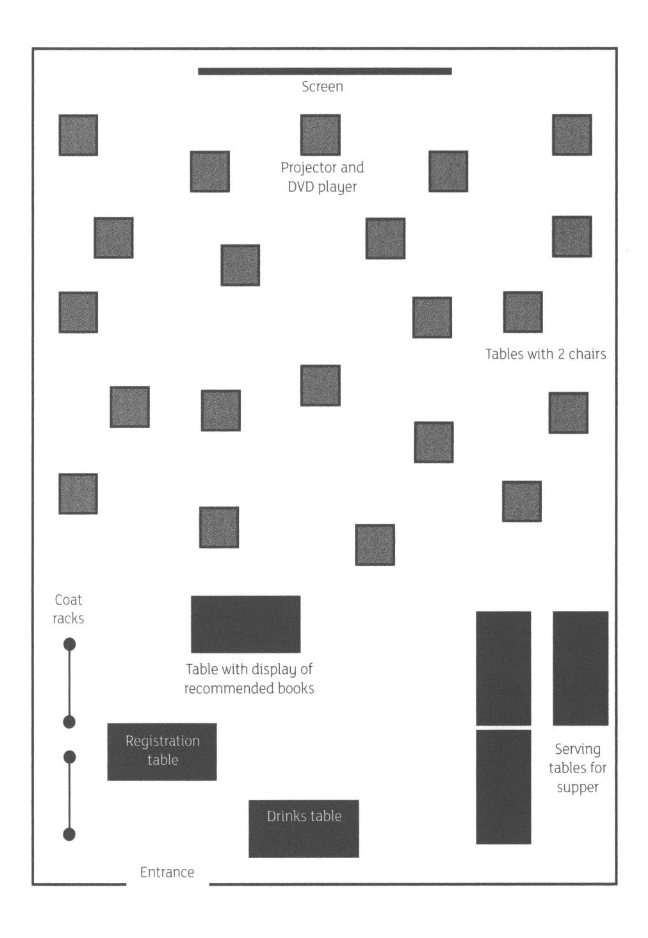

Contact information

Please feel free to contact us for more information or if we can be of assistance:

themarriagecourse.org
info@themarriagecourse.org
0845 644 75433

Other resources from Alpha International available from alphashop.org

Available to order from your local Christian bookshop, or from:
www.alphashop.org

Phone the Alpha Publications Hotline on
0845 758 1278 or **email alpha@stl.org**
To order from overseas: **+44 1228 611749**

themarriagecourse.org